The Business Partnership Survival Guide

How Siblings, Parents, Cousins, and Friends Get
On the Same Page to Build A Profitable Business

Nancy Jonker, PhD

Creator of the Audacious Leaders M.O. Program
Grand Rapids, Michigan, United States

Nancy Jonker, PhD
2707 Breton Rd. SE, Grand Rapids, Mich. 49549
Grand Rapids, Michigan 49546, United States
Nancyjonker.com

Ordering Information:
Quantity sales. Special discounts are available on quantity purchases by corporations, associations, and others. For details, contact the "Special Sales Department" at the address above.

Business Partnership Survival Guide /Nancy Jonker—1st ed.
ISBN: 978-1-7363208-0-8

TABLE OF CONTENTS

To my parents Gord and Marilyn and my siblings
Deb, Sandy, Kathy, Kristi, and David

Where Challenges and Opportunity Meet

Welcome to the Business Partnership Survival Guide. I know you're here for a good reason. Maybe you know there are inevitable challenges with partnerships, and you're looking ahead to prevent problems down the road.

Or, maybe you're in the thick of things, and you know there's got to be a better way to navigate through this. Either way, you've come to the right place. It's time to get on the same page so you can build a more profitable business.

Challenges Inherent in Any Partnership

Business partnerships are full of potential and promise. They offer an excellent opportunity to leverage diverse talents, to collaborate, to share the financial and emotional risks of running a business, and to have fun doing it.

But for any partnership or team, the opportunity for enrichment also involves challenges. As wonderful as business partnerships can be, they're tricky. And the irony is that the more meaningful the relationship is to you, the more likely it is that tensions will go underground.

Challenges Inherent in Family Business Partnerships

Business partnerships among family members bring their own set of challenges. Let's foray into developmental psychology for a minute. The task of maturation into adulthood often involves creating some distance and autonomy to do things your way as you differentiate from other family members.

This developmental task is often thwarted in a family business. It's hard to grow up in a family business and have parents or others in the business see and respect your full competence without feeling the need to constantly prove yourself.

Sons or daughters may 'chomp at the bit' wanting to use their skills to bring in more innovation, new technology, or people with different ideas. Without the freedom to do so, frustrations can go underground or become the source of frequent arguments.

And parents don't always have an easy time shifting their perspective and expectations of their kids. Even if they see their adult children as competent, they may not have the confidence to let go and let them function autonomously in their own lane.

On the other side, parents may not see clearly the ways their son or daughter struggles and isn't an ideal fit for the role they're occupying. And even when they do see the lack of fit, they may not know what to do. Family ties can conflict with business imperatives, and the parent in the business often feels caught in the middle.

Siblings, and to some extent cousins, may bring overtones of their childhood and teenage dynamics into the business. Again, this often occurs without much awareness until problems crop up and reveal some of these patterns at work.

No One Wants to Rock the Boat

When you have relationships you want to protect, it often seems much easier just to *avoid* conversations and the tension of having those conversations.

And when your business partner is your family member, it's not only you and your partner you're thinking about—it's the whole web of family relationships. Likewise, with a close friend, disruptions in the relationship can have a far-reaching impact on multiple areas of your life.

If you're like most business owners, you probably expect yourself to know how to manage the complexities of doing business with family members or friends and to do it *well* besides.

Whether you plunged in and expected to figure it out as you went along, or you took time in the beginning to lay a good foundation, you might be surprised at the challenges you face and how risky it feels to deal with them. Often when I talk to partners in a business, one or both of them asks the question, "how did we get here?"

The answer is that seemingly small things build up. You can let things go underground and override them for quite some time. But there always comes a time when the tensions become apparent and have to be addressed. And when partners fail to address those issues, the very sustainability of the business is at stake.

The time to be dealing with these issues is sooner rather than later because those unaddressed tensions and conflicts in your relationship aren't neutral. When you and your partner aren't on the same page, it's affecting your business in both big and small ways, and it's affecting your personal life too.

Might You Be That Frog?

Like the frog in a gradually heated pot of boiling water, you may reach a point where the stress begins to register. Maybe you notice it's sapping your energy, dampening your enthusiasm, and even prompting you to question if you want to continue with your partner or go your own way.

Yet you know that dissolving the partnership or walking away would have serious consequences for the business. And it would impact you and your partner and the web of multiple relationships you each have. So that's not an easy road even when it seems like the 'simpler' solution.

If you're like most people, when you don't know what to do to fix a problem, you'll push it down the road and do nothing at the moment, hoping things will get better or clearer as you go along.

A common alternative to doing nothing is to do *something*—anything at all—when a situation gets bad enough to trigger a reaction. Then you may be inclined to do *something*—like initiate a conversation or institute a new policy.

Those efforts are often unsuccessful because they come out of a place of exasperation or frustration— and that rarely sets the stage for working out a creative solution.

The cycle shown on the right is likely to reinforce the belief that it's too risky to talk about the issues, and it may send you and your partner back to your separate corners.

This cycle gets reinforced each time one of you does "something" without tending to the quality of the atmosphere and the foundations for a successful outcome.

So, if you haven't solved the challenges you and your partner face, take heart. You're not alone, and you're not to blame. You just haven't had a guide and a roadmap that lays out a clear and proven pathway to get you where you need to go.

The Roadmap You've Been Waiting For

The pages that follow contain that roadmap—a proven process to address the challenges ahead of you while protecting the relationships you care about. A process that allows each of you to come together with your best foot forward, calling to mind the reasons you embarked on this journey together in the first place.

What we're going to do is walk through the process step by step so you can be the kind of leader you've always wanted to be, address unspoken tensions safely, and get on the same page to build a more profitable business.

And what's more, you're going to see how much easier your life and running your business can be.

Your Very Own Magic Wand

I've learned over the years that most people don't just want a roadmap. What they *really* want is a magic wand. During my first year in private practice, I heard that wish expressed so often I went out and bought a beautifully decorated magic wand!

When I offered the wand to my clients, they knew immediately they were not alone in their wish! Then I'd tell them that this roadmap was the closest thing I knew to a magic wand—the way to get them the results they wanted with as much ease and speed as possible.

Because, of course, you're not here just for results. You want it to be easy, fast, and as smooth as possible with little or no risk. After all, no one wants to be worse off than they were before!

This approach comes as close to waving a magic wand as you can get. You see, this process is easier and more comfortable than most because it's deeply rooted in psychology and starts on the foundation of strengths.

Paving the Way for Change

Most of the preparation for change, the heavy lifting, if you will, is done on the inside where there's no risk involved. Because this method focuses on mindset and creating the change you want to see in the 'theater of your mind,' you can begin to roll out the changes you want in a very low-risk way.

How does that work? Either you or you and your partner focus on the internal process first and then come together when you feel ready to engage with your best foot forward. By this time, you will have set the stage for successful conversations to get you on the same page and help you solve problems as they arise.

Does that *actually* work, you might ask? Indeed it does. It's surprising that this style of creating change is not better known and practiced!

Let's move now to what things are like when you're not on the same page.

CHAPTER 1

What Out of Sync Leadership Is Like

C hances are, some of the signs that you and your partner aren't on the same page are things you're already experiencing.

You may have thought you were on the same page in the beginning, but as things continue to unfold, you may wonder if you ever did see eye to eye on some of these fundamental aspects of running a business. Or maybe you didn't want to talk about it then and hoped you might never have to. Or maybe you thought you'd be far enough along that it would be more comfortable as time went on.

But now, you may be becoming aware that you have a different set of values that propel you forward. You may have different ideas about what kind of culture you want to create and how to manage and reward people in the business. You may have different ideas about how to go about hiring and where and how to use resources most effectively.

You may experience a growing mistrust that your partner is looking out for the business's best interest and not putting their own interests or their family's needs first. You may not see eye to eye on when to act on opportunities you see—and maybe you can't even agree on what genuine options are out there.

You may also have a lack of clear and defined roles, and therefore you may not know when to act independently and when to collaborate. This ambiguity around roles can create a lot of redundant effort and put you in charge of things you're not good at or never wanted to do.

The Boat That Goes Around in Circles

When you don't agree on some of these fundamental things about running a business, it's like trying to row a boat that keeps going in circles. When partners don't coordinate their efforts, the boat can't move forward.

What that looks like in a business is that different kinds of problems start cropping up. You might see employees looking out more for themselves, showing less team spirit, or being less engaged. Eventually, you might find out that key team members are looking around for work opportunities elsewhere.

You might notice that the performance of either you or your partner goes down. You may see or experience perceptions of inequality, where there's a sense that things aren't fair or that people under-appreciate or under-reward your contributions. And you might see a growing lack of trust in each other's judgment.

The Boat that Fills with Water

We've already seen that no one wants to rock the

boat in partnerships with family and friends. Sometimes this means the boat goes around in circles while the leaders try to get in sync. But sometimes, the boat fills with water—threatening the sustainability of the journey.

In a business partnership, unchecked resentment may start to leak out in sarcasm, undermining comments about the partner in front of or to team members, or 'stealing time' away from the business. I call this the Cycle of the 3 R's that can repeat itself over and over, creating a self-perpetuating loop.

The Cycle of the 3 R's

Resentment

Remorse   **'Revenge'**

The cycle of the 3 R's—resentment, revenge, and remorse—locks partners in maladaptive patterns, unable to create the success they want. What does this cycle look like in action? Maybe something like this.

As you feel growing resentment or resignation, you might start engaging in small, subconscious, 'revenge-like' behaviors such as decreased performance that reflects your waning motivation. Or you might start taking more time away from the business because work feels so bad and you think you need more time to recover. But then you might also feel guilt or remorse, knowing you're not giving your all.

There are two consequences of this pattern. One is that feeling guilty motivates you to look for ways your partner is being difficult as a way to justify your behavior and even things out.

The other consequence has to do with your partner's reaction. If your partner has complaints about your level of commitment or activity in the business, this cycle will likely reinforce their perspective. Of course, this pattern could go the other way as well, where you're the one having your view of your partner reinforced.

This cycle tends to function underground, and you may not be aware of it at all until you check and see if this pattern is in play. If it is, it's likely to keep you locked into the status quo.

What's Happening to that Frog Anyway?

The problem of not being on the same page goes way beyond its effects on the business. When there's trouble in the leadership team, all kinds of ripple effects impact the partners. Things you might be experiencing even as you read this.

You might approach your work with a feeling of dread or feel like you have to be careful and tiptoe around. You might feel the heavy weight of decisions because you and your partner can't agree on things, so even though you want to take risks and move forward with opportunities, you feel like you have to be more conservative.

The problems between you and your partner are probably eating up your mental energy, too, gnawing at you during the day and keeping you awake at night. That negative energy weighs you down and affects the business and your leadership in it. You might see health issues that crop up or relationships at home that start to show the strain. You might hear more frequent complaints from your spouse or kids.

You might notice an uptick in irritability and exhaustion or that you're eating or drinking more than usual. You might feel constantly preoccupied with work, so much so that it interferes with being present for the daily joys of life. You might find yourself sneaking time away or hiding decisions you're making from your partner. And all the while, you might feel more and more like unsolvable problems or tensions weigh you down.

Contrast this scenario with what's possible when leaders are on the same page. We'll turn our attention now to the massive opportunities with 'same page leadership.' We'll use a case example to bring the material to life.

CHAPTER 2

Massive Opportunities with Same Page Leadership

When leaders are on the same page, the business can flow, work can feel energizing, and the partnership can feel supportive rather than stressful.

Now, if you've gotten worn down by the tensions and problems in your partnership, you might feel downright cynical about investing time and energy to make changes. It's understandable.

But just imagine for a moment that it's Friday afternoon, and while going over your weekly dashboard and enjoying your afternoon coffee, you feel a smile spread across your face as you see success across all measures.

Your team is moving in a unified direction. You, as partners, are using your unique talents and having productive conversations regularly. Team members are energized and committed, and customer satisfaction is strong.

Not only that, you've created a culture that makes it feel like a great place to work. Your business is stable and sustainable, plus you're ready to act on opportunities as they arise.

Not only do you have more time to work on the business doing work you enjoy and are good at, but you also have more time and energy to be with your family and friends and enjoy time on the court, the course, or the beach.

One of Those Frogs—A Real Life Example

The story of "Joe and Adam" illustrates this transformation. Joe is the little brother in the family business. He and his brother Adam inherited the business from their father and worked hard to sustain the company into the next generation.

At the time Joe contacted me, he was exhausted and frustrated. His wife complained that he was irritable whenever he was around and that he was of little help to her or the kids. (You know that story of being home, but not really 'being there.')

Joe was feeling overwhelmed and overworked. He would come home tired in the evening, but wouldn't know what to do to relax, so he'd drink and watch Netflix. By the time he wanted to sleep, his mind was in overdrive again.

Joe knew they were missing opportunities to grow the business, which just added to his frustration. Running the company was coming at a huge personal cost, and he was starting to look for a way out. He knew he couldn't match the income potential he had with the family business but didn't know what he could do to make his life more manageable.

The business was negatively affected, as well as Joe's health. Even though he and his brother wanted to grow the business, they couldn't agree on which opportunities to pursue, how quickly to act, or under what circumstances.

They also couldn't agree on how to manage the people who had been in the business for a long time. Joe wanted to have clear expectations and accountability, and Adam didn't want to ruffle feathers.

Joe and Adam are a good illustration of what happens when leaders aren't on the same page. Despite his efforts, Joe didn't know how to get to a more unified approach to leadership with Adam, especially because his brother saw no need for change.

Only Three Things You Need to Do to Get On The Same Page

The really good news is, there are only three things necessary for success:
1. Show up as your best self;
2. Set the stage for successful conversations;
3. Solve problems as they arise.

As you apply the steps of this roadmap, you'll have the resources to clear out anything within yourself that hinders your effective leadership. You'll reconnect to your vision and unload any personal baggage that interferes with you being your best self.

Second, you'll know how to lay the foundation for successful conversations so you can have them whenever needed and find effective resolutions.

And third, once you have that confidence and track record, you'll be in a position to solve problems as they arise rather than putting them off and allowing the tensions to build.

The Frog That Found Its Way Out—The Transformation

Joe was highly motivated to change his circumstances once he saw he had become the frog in boiling water. As he followed the three steps for success, he dramatically changed his life, partnership, and how the business functioned. More details about the actual process are provided in subsequent chapters, but here's the overview of Joe's journey to success.

First, to show up as his best self, Joe invested time in rekindling his vision for the business and his life. He actively envisioned the partnership he wanted in as much detail as he could. He discovered his 'story'— the narrative that kept him stuck in place and kept him and his brother on that never-ending merry-go-round of avoidance, tension, arguments, and resignation.

Joe discovered his strengths and learned that he was trying to lead in a way that didn't come naturally to him. He learned to spot when he was holding back and became more adept at monitoring his frustration and overwhelm.

To truly create fertile ground for change, Joe got crystal clear about how he was contributing to the situation he didn't like—including how he made it easy for others to dismiss him. He connected his current feelings with the experiences he had growing up in his family and gradually unloaded his 'emotional baggage.'

Then Joe honed his communication skills, finding ways to initiate conversations that ensured the best chances for success. He and Adam set time aside to talk about decisions they needed to make, so these issues didn't get pushed off or get handled when they were both tired or hurried.

Joe followed the five C's for successful conversations and found that, sure enough, he and his brother were able to talk about and solve topics that had previously resulted in angry eruptions or days of silence.

Finally, as diligence and attention to these personal and communication skills paid off, Joe and Adam developed a track record of resolving differences without major conflict. When issues arose that prompted disagreements, Joe and Adam solved them quickly before tensions escalated, making their partnership more resilient and their business more agile.

Just nine months later, Joe and Adam experienced a 25% growth in their business through a strategic acquisition. Their time and energy, formerly spent on troubleshooting, was now spent on innovation.

They had clear expectations and processes for their people to follow, and performance improved across the board. Customer satisfaction was high (like award-winning high), and they were clear about their roles. Joe and Adam were productive in their own lanes knowing when to check in with each other and when to move forward using their own judgment.

CHAPTER 3

But Wait! What If This Won't Work for Me?

Y ou might be thinking to yourself, all well and good for Joe and Adam or others like them who have a situation more amenable to change—partners who aren't as mired in problems as we are or who have dealt with things earlier.

Before you conclude that this process won't work for you, look at some of the common questions business partners raise. Maybe one or more applies to you.

What If My Partner Wants to Keep Rowing the Boat Even though It's Going in Circles?

It's frequently the case that one partner is more motivated and ready for change than both partners being ready and motivated at the same time. Sometimes it happens that both people cross the tolerance threshold simultaneously. But more often than not, it's one person who not only sees the problems but is willing (and sometimes desperate enough) to be the agent of change.

If you are the partner initially motivated toward change, you're going to discover ways to step into your full capacity as a leader. You're going to see the mental models that have been operating in the background. You'll become aware of your own mental barriers that have contributed to the situation you find yourself in.

Most of us have far more power than we think. We often don't see the actions we're taking as coming out of our belief system and don't see how our expectations impact how *we* engage and how our partner engages with us.

There's lots of research that supports this. When teachers have higher expectations of their students, those students perform at higher levels. When parents have higher expectations of their kids, their kids often rise to those expectations. When we have expectations for successful outcomes with our partners, we're far more likely to see those successful outcomes than when our expectations are low.

This is true even when our low expectations are born out of repeated experiences. When we're looking to change things, not to perpetuate more of what is and has been, it's important to let go of expectations born out of the past and open to the possibility for change.

The roadmap presented here works even if you're the only partner willing and motivated to engage, even if you're full of doubt. Even if you're not sure how motivated and resilient you feel—that's when it's needed the most and when you reap the most benefit.

How Do I Convince My Partner to Change Course?

This is a variation of the above and tends to be the question almost every dissatisfied business partner asks. The way forward isn't apparent when your partner either doesn't see a need for change (maybe it's working well enough for them) or is unwilling to make the necessary accommodations that would serve the partnership and business.

How do you convince them to change?

You don't!

Trying to change them or get them to change is a losing enterprise and a recipe for frustration. So what to do?

You focus on every aspect of life and leadership within your sphere of influence (more on this later). In time, your partner will not be able to 'do the status quo' because the status quo will have shifted dramatically.

What if I'm desperate to get off this sinking ship?

Even if you think the best solution might be for you to exit or sell the business, chances are good you want to do that from a position of strength. First of all, it's hard to make a clear and great decision when you're feeling beaten down and your vision for the business is tarnished.

Frequently, partners in this kind of situation are disappointed, disillusioned, angry, or resentful. Deciding to sell or leave from that state of mind doesn't set the foundation for a successful outcome or the most successful transition into your next chapter.

So even if you're looking to bring the business to a close or to exit as a partner, it pays to do so from a strong position. And doing so in a way that builds your resilience and protects relationships to the greatest extent possible is key. The way to do that is to follow this very same roadmap.

What if I don't have time or money to fix the boat right now?

This is also a common occurrence. There never seems to be a good time for business partners to take a step back and address what's going on. The demands of the business are urgent and often endless. Plus, when there's tension or fear of rocking the boat, it truly never seems like the right time.

But it's important to look at what it costs you in terms of the overwhelm you feel every day, the inefficiency of how you spend your days, and your reduced effectiveness.

There are huge opportunity costs when leaders aren't on the same page. You're not the leader you know you have the capacity to be, and you're not getting your team members' best efforts. There's nothing for your employees to get behind to motivate their own efforts when there's no unified vision or strategy. Plus, deep down, you know you're not functioning at your peak performance, and neither is your partner.

All of these are costs to the business that occur each day. And until you're able to address and fix the issues between you and your partner and get on the same page, they will not get better.

CHAPTER 4

Maximize Your Ability to Create the Solutions You Want

Chances are when you encountered challenges in your partnership and business, the vision that you had in the beginning, started to dim.

All the problems may have chipped away at your dream, dulling its brilliance and taking the shine off of what you once thought was possible. There's a gap now between what you dreamed of and the current reality. It can be uncomfortable, even a little depressing, to revisit your dreams and acknowledge that your situation doesn't come close to what you hoped for your business.

Dwell in Possibility to Rekindle Your Vision

The first thing to do is to take a deep breath, take a figurative step back, and begin to think about what's possible. I call this 'dwelling in possibility.'

In order to reconnect to your vision, dwell in possibility, and think creatively again about what's possible, you'll need to be able to manage the emotions that come up as you realize the gap between what you hoped for and what is.

This is where mindset and resilience become essential.

Most people don't spend enough time in this envisioning part. They're quick to focus on the problems and not think enough about what they'd like to experience instead.

When you connect to the vision of what could be, it's helpful to break it down into its parts. For example, when you take your overarching goal of building a profitable business, it's useful to envision the specific details.

Separate but related goals are key to reaching overall success. Milestones along the way, such as smooth operations, having customers call or write in to tell you how happy they are with your service, and having a shared strategy of holding people accountable and rewarding them for their efforts, motivate you toward your overarching goals.

To clarify the smaller aspects of your overall vision, it's helpful to answer the following questions.

- What are the things that give your day meaning and provide you a sense of accomplishment?
- When you wake up in the morning, how do you want to feel about going to work?
- How do you want your day to flow?
- What do you want to look forward to?
- What kind of exchanges do you want to have with your partner(s)?
- What do you want the outcome of a 'good conversation' to be?
- Do you want to start your days with a daily check-in? Do you want to set up other habits or patterns to create a sense of rapport and trust?

One other important aspect of vision worth mentioning here is taking some time to reassess your values. It's so helpful to know what matters to you and why. It's hard to envision the life that you want and what part your business plays in that when you don't know what *really* matters to you.

Taking a quick values inventory or revisiting the values assessments you've already done is another way to reconnect to your vision. There are some great online tools for this. Or simply reviewing a list of values and circling the ones that matter to you, and then paring them down to three to five or even seven will help you understand what motivates you in your business and what you want to focus on in moving forward.

The Theater that's Always Open

The other important part of rekindling your vision is to begin creating in the 'theater of your mind' the change you want to see. This is where change first occurs, and this theater is always open for you! You can create whatever you want to see and experience there because you have full control in this arena.

There is ample evidence that mental rehearsal produces physical changes, much like engaging in the action itself. Olympic athletes use this technique with great effect.

The brain doesn't distinguish between what's happening in one's mind internally and what's happening in the physical world externally. This is why mindset matters so much and why you want to monitor what you 'replay' in your mind's eye.

As you create this powerful 'mental movie' of what you want your life and relationships to look like, I suggest you create an IMAX version, so you're immersed in the experience. Better yet, create the extrasensory version, including all your senses as you generate mental movies of how you want your relationship and business to be.

In your mental movies, incorporate small milestones such as how you feel when you see your partner and how you feel when talking to each other. Envision with all your senses the great feeling that you have at the end of the discussion, or feeling elated when you've been able to clearly articulate your interests, lead with curiosity, and listen to your partner's perspective.

Most people ignore the 'theater of the mind' and don't use their imagination to enlist their power to change. But since you know how powerful and important it is, you can begin to harness this incredible tool without further delay.

Now that you see how taking a step back and dwelling in possibility can create the breathing room and space you need for change; we move on to the next step of developing a stellar mindset.

CHAPTER 5

Owning the Problem to Create Unlimited Solutions

I f you're like most people, when you're up against a tough problem, it's easier to attribute the source of the problem to something outside of yourself.

"He's the problem... and he won't change. Not that I'm perfect, but ..."

I've heard some variation of this time and again.

No matter what the specifics are—whether it's that he won't listen when you try to innovate, or she's not open to more efficient methods, or he won't adopt clear KPI's for the team and hold them accountable—it's easier to point at what your partner is or isn't doing than to see how you're contributing to the problems by what you're doing or not doing.

Yet, it opens up huge possibilities for change when you accept that a good portion of the problem is how you're acting or reacting to the problems you perceive with your partner.

Which Image Best Describes You?

If you're not convinced that at least part of the battle is *within you*, picture in your mind's eye, these two different images of yourself.

One, you're like a fish covered with scales. Remarks made to you or about you *hook* you—they *get under your skin,* and you have a hard time not retorting in anger, withdrawing, or becoming ridden with guilt. Or, you become so exasperated with your partner, so resigned, or so uncertain of what to do that you're constantly stressed, exhausted, and overwhelmed.

Two, you're like a teflon pan. Nothing triggers you; nothing sticks to you; nothing creates defensiveness. Derogatory comments come your way and slide right down to the ground. This isn't false invincibility; it's having unloaded enough of your own baggage that you become non-reactive to things that used to trigger you. You can stay calm and centered as you deal with the challenges at hand.

Note that even non-emotionally reactive partners have their limits. At some point, the business or the partnership may not warrant the level of work you need to do to stay clean and clear.

When you've cleared away your baggage and know your triggers and how to resolve them, you're in a much better position to make decisions and plans for the future.

Use The 0/100 Rule to Be in the Driver's Seat

The stellar mindset you want to have starts with the "0/100 rule of responsibility." This means that you take 100% responsibility for everything in your realm—your motivations, actions, intentions, outcomes of your actions, what you do, what you say, how you say it, what you don't say, and why. Whew! That's quite a list. And the flip side of this is that you take zero percent responsibility for your partner.

When I tell my clients that the challenge is for them to take 100% responsibility for themselves and 0% responsibility for their partners, they're often taken aback. They think that they're getting some sort of a deal or that it's a cop-out or a way of being less considerate of their partner.

In truth, though, it's the most accountable framework you could set up for yourself. You don't get off the hook for anything. If you say something with a sarcastic tone of voice, that's yours. If you avoid having conversations because you're uncomfortable, that's yours too. If you're reactive to something, your partner said because of your own history, that's on you.

Maybe this seems tricky or confusing. Maybe you know about the self-fulfilling prophecy phenomenon and know that if your partner reacts badly to you, you had something to do with it. And indeed, you did. The task is to review the experience in a self-reflective, non-emotional way to parse out what was yours and what was theirs.

Use the *Responsibility Grid* to Get Instant Clarity

The *Responsibility Grid* is a tool I created to help partners sort out what they are and are not responsible for. It's simple to make your own. Take a sheet of paper and about a third of the way down (leaving room to write at the top) draw a line down the center of the page to create two columns, and write on the left side, "Mine," and on the right side, write "Not Mine."

Then, review the interaction in a neutral, matter-of fact way, taking out emotion and simply writing down what happened. The next step is to separate which aspects you were and were not responsible for, placing them in the appropriate column.

For example, Jack and Jill, co-owners of the business, have an interaction over determining budget items for the next year, and it ends in a shouting match. Since Jill is the partner initially invested in making changes, there are many segments for her to get clear on. Let's unpack it.

Jill approached Jack on the fly, and when she was in a hurry, even though she knew this would be a delicate conversation. That's hers. When asked about a particular budget item, she got defensive. That's hers. When Jack heard her defensiveness, he clamped down harder. That's his. Jill responded in anger. That's hers. And Jack, in his exasperation, began shouting. That's his. Jill shouted back and walked away in anger. That's hers.

When Jill parses out each element of the interaction this way, she can see where she can change her behavior and improve the odds for a successful conversation and outcome. More about this in chapter 9.

Getting clear about each element of an interaction (even if it's you avoiding the interaction) frees you up to take control over the large number of things in your own arena. It also frees you from trying to exert control over something that you're not in charge of, that you have no control over. (Control is different from influence.)

It's a bit of a paradox. The more you stop trying to control others, the more ability you have to produce real change in your realm of responsibility. The effect is to put you in the driver's seat of your life and influence more aspects of the business than you ever realized you could impact.

Let Go of Stories and Monitor Meanings to Build a Stellar Mindset

Another way to be in the driver's seat of your life and build a stellar mindset is to let go of your 'story.' Stories are narratives you repeat to yourself that can keep you stuck in limiting beliefs and unproductive patterns of relating.

Stories remain active and alive through the meaning we give our experiences. We see events through the lens of our existing beliefs and ignore the parts of reality that don't fit with those beliefs. In doing so, we perpetuate unconscious stories about ourselves, others, and the way the world works.

Stories about ourselves include beliefs about what keeps us safe, what gives us worth, and whether we're lovable or not. Stories about others can be broad assumptions such as that people are out for themselves, that rich people are snobs, or that people don't understand. Stories about how the world works include things like money is hard to make, hard work pays off, or people get what they deserve.

In partnerships, we not only act out stories about ourselves, but create stories about our partners as well. It's common to attribute motives, attitudes, and meaning about their behavior that often have far more to do with us than with them. For example, Joe had a story about how his brother didn't take him seriously or give him credit for his ideas. As the younger brother in his family, he had actual historical data! His experiences growing up told him this was true.

With some help, Joe was able to see that his experiences as a kid were influencing the ways he perceived and reacted to events today. He wasn't aware that he was interacting in ways that made it easy for his brother to dismiss him, such as suggesting his ideas in an off-hand way, almost as if he didn't believe in them himself.

Most of the time we don't notice our stories operating in the background, shaping our perspective. We don't pause and ask, "What actually happened here? Am I projecting an old story about myself or of them?" or "What are the facts? Where might I be attaching a meaning that isn't actually true?"

This is where the *Meaning Monitor* can be helpful. Just like with the *Responsibility Grid*, you can *deconstruct the neutral experience from the meaning you've given it*. This helps you identify the distortions that creep in that are part of your story.

To make your own *Meaning Monitor*, take a sheet of paper and draw two lines down the page, creating three columns. Label the left column, "Neutral Event," label the middle column, "My Interpretation/Meaning" and label the right column, "Other Possible Meanings." In the left column, write down what happened, being as neutral as possible, sticking to objective facts. In the next column, write down the meaning you gave the event. In the right column, make a list of other possible meanings or interpretations.

For example, if Joe were using the *Meaning Monitor*, he would write in the left column "Adam didn't respond to my email for three days." In the center column, he might write "He doesn't take me seriously;" and "My suggestions are a low priority for him." In the right column, Joe might list these possibilities, "Adam was busy with other things;" "Adam needed time to think about the suggestions I made in my email;" "Adam doesn't have an efficient way of tracking and managing emails."

Once you see alternative meanings for events, you can see how you perpetuate your story with your subjective interpretation of events. Developing the capacity to see this helps build a stellar mindset and opens new avenues for change.

Show Up as Your Best Authentic Self

Doing the work around mindset can shift your reality in powerful ways. When you're *aware,* you can challenge your stories, transform your limiting beliefs, and monitor the meaning you give to your experiences to create new patterns of thinking and relating.

Awareness is key. However, our awareness is inherently limited, much as a driver's perspective is limited by blind spots. Just as drivers rely on cameras and mirrors to eliminate blind spots, individuals and partners can use outside perspectives to illuminate mental models and stories that are operating in the background—complete with assumptions, limiting beliefs, and unexpressed expectations.

Building your stellar mindset through frequent use of the *Responsibility Grid,* the *Meaning Monitor,* and an outside perspective allow you to show up as your best self. You're able to respond to your partners from a clean and clear perspective—more like the teflon pan and less like the fish that is easily 'hooked.'

Each time you see a pattern that isn't healthy or productive, ask yourself: *Who do I need to be to bring about the change I want to see? How do I need*

45

to show up and interact to make this change more likely? Then *visualize* this. Now you're ready to take action with your partner and create unlimited solutions.

CHAPTER 6

The Learning Approach Advantage for Continual Success

Another aspect of mindset is to take a learning approach into all of our experiences. Some might call this a gaming attitude; others might call it a growth mindset. The idea is to allow ourselves to experiment and hold the position that we are always succeeding because even when things don't turn out the way we expected or hoped, we learn from it.

When we can adopt this growth, learning, and experimentation attitude, we create space for ourselves to grow, learn, and succeed.

The impact of these mindset tools cannot be overstated; when you're willing to take full responsibility for your entire experience, it impacts how you interact with others. Then you can approach your life with an attitude of learning. The world truly opens up with possibilities following this new mindset.

Just feel how much easier it is to breathe when you think about everything that can be possible. And notice how you can harness that just by spending time thinking about those possibilities and creating them in your mind's eye.

The Transformative Triangle

The Transformative Triangle is how leaders live into their vision and full responsibility *without shrinking or shirking.* It's how you can show up as the best version of yourself. How does this work?

Practice being audacious, gracious, and tenacious.

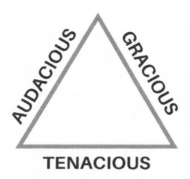

TENACIOUS

Be Audacious—the First Facet of the Transformative Triangle

What might it look like if you were to be audaciously yourself? My guess is that you might show up as a different kind of leader. You would speak your mind. You would lead from both a powerful and vulnerable position.

You would spend time knowing your opinions about the way things work in the business, the financial picture, the way you want to reward people on your team, and how you want to measure success.

When you're audacious, you would venture outside of your comfort zone and not avoid difficult conversations. And you would not retreat from things that you strongly believe.

Another part about being audacious is setting and maintaining great boundaries around your time and energy. When you know what's important to you and are willing to protect what matters to you, you're able to create clarity and effectiveness.

When you're clear about your boundaries, you can communicate them with grace, and you can tenaciously stick to them so that you can create what you want in the world.

If you can get outside of your comfort zone and be willing to show up as your full and authentic self, you create the freedom for others to do that too.

Be Gracious—the Second Facet of the Transformative Triangle

Audaciousness must be coupled with graciousness to be effective. This is a powerful combo. When you can show up as your authentic self, you can express yourself with grace.

When you stop showing up as your authentic self and allow feelings and opinions to go underground (even when well-intentioned), that's when sarcasm, exasperation, or frustration begins to leak out.

People are often mean or sarcastic or unthinking in their interactions when they've been holding back. When partners tolerate what they perceive to be inequities, when they try to override their own opinions 'for the good of the relationship,' they become susceptible to the 'exasperated parent' phenomenon. When an exasperated parent has been tolerating behavior they don't like and then finally says (yells) something, it's usually **not** done with grace.

Be Tenacious—the Third Facet of the Transformative Triangle

Being audacious and gracious are two aspects of the transformative triangle. The third is to be tenacious. This involves being willing to stay in conversation until there's clarity, continuing to approach your partner with curiosity until you have some understanding of their perspective.

It's also a willingness to go the extra mile to not only understand your differing points of view but to reach some sort of agreement about how to proceed.

I often see people taking a stab at having a conversation or gaining clarity, but they back away when things get tough. Usually, this reinforces their conclusion that they can't talk about things or can't resolve issues.

So tenaciousness—a willingness and an ability to stick with the process long enough to achieve a resolution—is also necessary.

If you're like most partners, you already have one or two of these aspects well in hand, but would benefit from developing, and even emphasizing for a time, the other one or two.

For example, if you're already gracious in your conversations and are tenacious as the day is long, you would do well to add audaciousness to the mix. Likewise, if you already show up audaciously, you might want to experiment with being more gracious and tenacious.

When you live into your vision and responsibility without shrinking or shirking and create a balance between audacity, grace, and tenacity, you lay the foundation for a whole new level of success.

CHAPTER 7

Being Savvy with Your Use of Strengths

The approach described in this roadmap is different because, rather than starting with the conflicts or tensions, we begin with the vision and discovery of strengths.

However, it's become clear to me over the years that people have an inherent distrust of assessments—even strengths assessments. They brace almost upon hearing the word. And I get it.

We've all been recipients of poorly delivered 'constructive feedback' or assessment results that tell us all the things that are wrong about us or need improvement.

Even when I type the word 'strengths' into the computer, what's automatically generated is the phrase '*and weaknesses*' as though that's the rest of my sentence.

People are accustomed to this package deal—you get to hear about your strengths but only in the context of your weaknesses. I believe this does a real disservice to people. We attach to the negative and miss the constructive part. It's just how the brain works.

New Discoveries and 'Conversational Grease'

In our Strengths Discovery Sessions, we focus exclusively on strengths. Why? Because it increases receptivity and helps us learn. We already have neural bundles in the areas of our strengths, which help us acquire new knowledge and move forward without reservation.

Partners benefit by communicating first about strengths and styles because there's a buffer between them, and they can use *data* to look more objectively at themselves and each other. The instinctive talents we focus on are not commonly known, so there's a real discovery involved.

Starting with a discussion about strengths also lowers defenses and provides 'conversational grease' to reduce friction in later conversations.

Having a real 'Strengths Discovery Session' is a uniquely different experience for most people. It's an experience I wish for you.

Capitalize on Natural Talents

When business owners don't understand their own and their partner's strengths, work style, and what work energizes them versus drains them, they don't have a clear basis for determining roles and responsibilities.

Furthermore, they don't have a framework to understand their differences, or the unfulfilled expectations they have of their partner.

When you don't understand your partner's natural style of solving problems, you're likely to attribute the differences between you as personality conflicts or even misattribute bad intentions to your partner.

For example, if you have a particular way of solving problems, and your partner's hard-wired approach is quite different, but you don't understand that, you might feel like they're dismissing you, or that they don't value your input, or that they don't care about what you think. In actuality, they're likely just taking action in the way that's most natural for them.

When I work with business partners, and even one of them becomes illuminated about their working style and how it differs from their partner's, it's as if they're playing Connect Four in their heads! They replay their interactions over the months and years with this new understanding, making a profound difference in how they think about their partner, their partner's contributions, and their own contributions.

Partners who discover their hard-wired approach to creating solutions and have access to their strengths in *all three parts of the mind* enjoy new insights that contribute to an expanded sense of possibility.

Clarify Roles Using the Three Parts of the Mind

You may not know anything about the three parts of the mind. I was a psychologist for almost twenty-five years before I learned about it!

You are likely aware of at least two parts of the mind—the cognitive and affective realms. You're probably also well-acquainted with the various ways of measuring your cognitive skills (your abilities, expertise, knowledge, and skills) and your affective proclivities (your personality, values, motivations, and preferences).

But chances are you're not familiar with the *conative* realm—the *doing* realm—the way you instinctively take action when working to solve problems and create solutions.

In the context of business, all three realms are important. In the *thinking realm*, skills, knowledge, and expertise are important qualifications for various types of work. In the *feeling realm*, personality, preferences, values, and attitudes are important when assessing a cultural fit and leadership potential and style.

57

In the *doing* realm, knowing what people will or won't do when they're free to do things their way, the make-up of their mental energy and instinctive strengths is important when fitting roles to different people and ensuring that work tasks are energizing rather than stressful and depleting.

Many people aren't aware that there's a way to measure our intuitive way of creating solutions, so most business partners are operating in the dark—not only regarding their own strengths and style but also their partner's strengths and style.

If you're willing to discover your strengths and especially look at how you approach creating solutions, you're going to have a whole new way to work effectively with your partner.

You're going to have a way to assign roles and responsibilities that fit you and your natural ways of working. You're going to find work that energizes you rather than drains you, and you'll be able to clarify who should be doing which tasks in the business.

You'll understand when to collaborate and when to work independently. Using strengths to clarify your roles and responsibilities, you can become so much more efficient and effective.

Savviness Around Strengths and Style Exemplified

Joe and his brother Adam's story is an excellent example of how important it is to understand a partner's strengths in all three parts of the mind.

We learned that in the *doing* realm, Joe was trying to fit in and do things the way Adam did them rather than doing things his own way. For example, instead of brainstorming new solutions and trying them out, he would research what had been done before and write proposals for the next steps.

This not only killed his momentum, it also contributed to his exhaustion, frustration, and overwhelm. Joe was going against his grain every day—working hard but seeing few results for his efforts and stressing him out in the process.

When Joe got clear about what his problem-solving style was and how it was different from Adam's, they were able to separate out better fitting roles for themselves. Adam focused on legal and other in-depth areas of work. Joe focused on working with the sales team, fostering relationships with vendors, and developing innovative products and services.

Joe and Adam found ways to work that fit their natural style and engaged in work that energized them rather than depleted them. This was a large part of what enabled them to grow their business and revenue successfully.

Everyone benefits from knowing their unique talents and leveraging them in a way that maximizes energy, efficiency, and enjoyment. And when you discover your strengths and styles, you can detangle the sources of conflict in your partnership and defuse them through greater awareness. What a game-changer!

CHAPTER 8

What Are the Essential Skills for Any Successful Partnership?

E ssential skills for any successful partnership include:

- Self-awareness—knowing who you are in your core, knowing what you think, value, and believe;

- Self-reflection—gaining insights into what drives you and how you impact those around you;
- Inner balance—allowing you to handle challenges and difficult conversations with stability and calm;
- Effective boundaries—guarding your time and energy and establishing and using 'rules of engagement' for productive communication.

Let's take a deeper look at each of these.

Know Thyself

Self-awareness is the foundation for emotional intelligence and is necessary for successful conversations. Self-awareness involves an element of self-reflection and mastery.

You need self-awareness to know when you're triggered and when you need to activate your inner balance. You need self-awareness to understand what you're feeling, and you need self- and other-awareness to observe how you're coming across to people. You need self-awareness to track your reactions and work them through in a productive way.

The Tool No Business Partner Should Be Without

Self-awareness is enhanced by use of a three-way mirror. What's that? A mirror? Yes...

When you're embedded in your way of thinking and entangled in conflicts with your partner, you need an outside perspective to help you see what you cannot.

It's a proverbial problem of not being able to see the forest for the trees. Or the picture that can't see its own frame. Part of this is perspective, and part is the inability to see your blind spots. You simply can't see the back of your own head.

Why Is Having A Mirror So Important?

When looking for solutions to problems, you need to frame the issue with enough accuracy and flexibility to foster a creative solution—one you haven't seen yet. This necessitates gaining a broader perspective.

A pad of paper and pen or a journal can function as a mirror, reflecting back to you the underpinnings of your thought processes. Taking *time* for self-reflection is half the battle. Jotting notes to yourself, journaling in paragraph form, or using an 'audible journal' on your smartphone can foster significant insights into your strengths, emotional reactions, defensive patterns, and so on.

Another person can also function as a mirror, reflecting back to you what you're not able to see yourself. In my experience, this person needs to be clean, clear, and reliable—someone *without a stake in the game* who has honed their ability to reflect back what they see *without distortion.* (You've probably visited fun houses around Halloween and seen the effects of distorted mirrors.)

When the conflicts between you distort the feedback your partner provides, it's all the more important to get a reliable and accurate reflection of your thinking and behavior beyond what team members or a spouse can provide. It's time to start using the right mirror!

Develop Your Tuned Mass Damper

In addition to self-awareness and reflection, you need inner balance and resilience. Inner balance allows you to move through the challenges of the day in a calm, unruffled way, being both stable and dynamic.

One way to think about inner balance is to use the metaphor of contemporary skyscrapers. For these buildings to withstand the forces of winds and earthquakes, engineers insert a 'tuned mass damper' into the core of the building's interior to absorb seismic shock.

There are videos where you can watch the big gold ball (the tuned mass damper) move as it absorbs the shock. The sway in the skyscraper is imperceptible as the counterforce in the core of the building absorbs the shifting ground's impact.

You need your own tuned mass damper that absorbs fluctuations and exerts a counterforce, dampening your reactivity and helping you respond to interpersonal and business challenges in a thoughtful, non-reactive way.

Mindfulness is another way to describe this process where you neither minimize the challenges nor catastrophize and make them worse than they are. When you function out of a sense of inner balance with mindfulness, you're in a position to take effective action.

Mend Broken or Missing Fences

I often use the metaphor of fences when talking

about boundaries. It's no surprise that business owners need to be good at erecting fences around tasks so their time and energy are available for their on top priorities.

But fences in partnerships with family and friends are essential—and more often ignored. Since there's already an existing relationship, partners frequently neglect to make the extra effort of establishing 'rules of engagement' whenever talking about business matters.

When partners fail to establish clear boundaries around the business, the field is wide open for old patterns and dysfunctional ways of talking to dominate—especially when tensions escalate.

For example, suppose family members are used to freely expressing their feelings in whatever manner suits them. Suppose no one establishes rules of engagement to ensure professionalism and respect within the business. In that case, family members may express anger, outrage, or resentment in ways *totally* inappropriate in a business setting.

When disrespect and anger sneak into business communication, it causes disruption and discomfort for everyone. Sometimes it gets so uncomfortable that valuable team members seek employment elsewhere just to get away from the palpable tension.

In times of conflict, boundaries that may have been intact at one time can erode. Maybe you've found yourself or your partner talking more and more flippantly, curtly, or like hormonal teenagers who forget they have a culture to maintain and a business to run.

Why Aren't Boundaries Managed More Effectively?

One reason partners don't manage these boundaries more effectively may be that they honestly don't know how important they are. Another reason may be that no one taught how to do it effectively.

Finally, people need a time and a place to work through the reactions they have. When partners 'override' their reactions for too long, these attitudes are bound to leak out.

In businesses with family members, issues such as sibling rivalry, resentment about experiences through the years, and unresolved family baggage often come into the business by default. There's simply no other way or place to process them. These old, unresolved tensions can threaten the survival of the company.

Mismanagement of boundaries is a primary reason business partners fail to resolve issues between them.

They either don't talk about things they know need to be addressed in the business (avoidance) or talk without having proper safeguards in place.

Safeguards can be as simple as an agreement to treat each other with respect and professionalism rather than condescension or disdain. Sometimes more comprehensive safeguards are warranted, such as having a third-party present when talking about subjects that are known to be difficult, where partners have a tendency either to escalate tensions or withdraw from arguments in anger and resignation.

Rules of engagement and other safeguards can be documented, so everyone is clear about expectations and boundaries—more on this in chapter 11.

CHAPTER 9

Implementing the Five C's of Successful Conversations

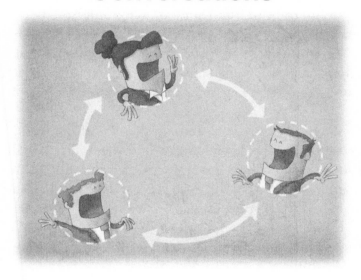

One of the primary challenges business partners face is having successful and clarifying conversations. And the irony is, the more significant the relationship, the harder this kind of communication can be. Not always, of course, but often.

When there's a strong interest in not rocking the boat or making matters worse, partners are more likely to hold back on the things they'd like to say. Then issues such as perceptions of inequality, objections to managerial style, or questions about procedures are likely to go underground.

Successful conversations require clarity of your own thoughts and openness to your partner. They need an ability to both listen and talk with emotional non-reactivity and grace. Many things can trigger a desire to defend ourselves, explain, or have someone see things from our perspective. But conversations with any or all of these agendas most often fall flat.

Having the courage to initiate conversations around even the touchiest of subjects and the ability to talk issues through and resolve conflict quickly is the main differentiator between successful and unsuccessful partnerships.

It is here that your essential skills for partnership *really* shine.

Starting with the Red Badge

The starting place for successful conversations is within you and begins with Courage. Being afraid to rock the boat is ultimately about fear. Fear of making things worse. Fear of getting caught in limbo with no clear resolution in sight. Fear of losing things valuable to you. Fear of rejection.

The list could go on, but you get the point. So first, you recognize the fear that's present, then muster your courage. Knowing you're prepared and have the skills necessary for these conversations is a good confidence booster, but it still requires making the decision to move forward with courage.

To Be or Not To Be

The second important step to implement in these all-important conversations is Choice. Besides having a choice about *whether* to have a conversation, you have multiple options for *how* to have these conversations.

You get to set the stage, choose your environment, the timing, and the safeguards to have in place. Once you know your partner's strengths, you can choose to tailor your mode of communication so it's easier for your partner to receive.

Having a choice also means you can stop negative patterns before they start. With the example of Jack and Jill, Jill could play the status quo scenario out in her mind and see where she'll end up. Then she can choose a different approach without ever having to have that unfavorable exchange.

This is how you improve your capacity to solve conflicts quickly and as they arise. You know how to avoid the dead ends because you know how to set the stage for success.

Bad for the Cat but Good for Your Partnership

The third C for fostering successful conversations is Curiosity. When you're curious, you let go of fear and your need to explain yourself. You set aside your point of view so you can be genuinely open to your partner's experience.

When you approach your partner with curiosity, you have a fighting chance of truly hearing their opinions and perspective.

When you're not leading with curiosity, you're living in the web of your assumptions and past experience. Your mental models, filled with your assumptions and belief system, take up all of your mental space, not allowing anything else to flow in.

Genuine curiosity has an aspect of humility in it. You don't pretend to know everything, and you give your partner space—even to be different from before. It's another way of opening to and dwelling in possibility.

The Appreciable Difference between Focused and Fuzzy

The fourth C for successful conversations is Clarity of message. Notice that curiosity precedes clarity about what you want to say. What you want to say is important, but seeking to understand first through an attitude of curiosity is even more critical.

To have clarity in your message, you need to describe what you want to say and why you want to say it. Knowing your mind—your beliefs, thoughts, and opinions and the values they're rooted in—provides the starting point for clear communication.

Next is to do a quick scan to assess your ego involvement and investment level in *your* point of view. Too much investment clouds your message, bringing overtones of unacknowledged emotion or a personal agenda that your partner may pick up and become skeptical about what you have to say.

A clear message achieves the balance of communicating what you want to say with enough tact and openness that your partner can hear it and take it in.

One reason partners might avoid being straightforward in their message is they're afraid of the reaction they'll get. They may hold back from saying what they think out of a fear of rejection or criticism. Maybe you've heard yourself say something like, "it's just not worth the fight."

This indicates two issues. One is that you're anticipating the reactions you're *afraid* to hear rather than envisioning the responses you *want* to hear. The other is that you can't lead with curiosity and openness if you already feel defeated and assume you know what your partner's reaction will be.

Clearing out your own emotional baggage and agenda first allows you to have greater clarity in your message, not to mention greater receptivity to your partner's response. How to gain more clarity or clear out your own stuff? Writing for ten minutes or so (you don't even need to read it when you're done) can be a hugely beneficial exercise.

Using the *Threshold Technique* to Increase Positive Results

Using what I call the *Threshold Technique* creates an opening for dialogue, reducing defensiveness and improving the odds for a successful outcome. It's essentially having a 'pre-conversation' with your partner *about* the conversation you want to have.

Rather than being preoccupied about how to talk about a sensitive topic or avoiding it all together, you simply voice your concerns about the upcoming discussion and your hope for a positive outcome. It's easy for your partner to be receptive to this approach.

For example, if you want to have a conversation with your partner about how they're handling performance issues—and you're concerned about the way it will be received—you can *preface the discussion* with—"I'd like to talk with you about how we're managing performance issues, and I'm concerned about how it's going to go. I respect your work and appreciate that you're handling these issues, **and** I want to make sure we're on the same page going forward."

This technique allows you to take action, but with preparation and intention ahead of time. These safeguards improve the likelihood for a successful outcome.

Communicating A Single Message for Maximum Effectiveness

The fifth C for successful conversations is Congruence. When you communicate with congruence, your whole self is unified in what you say and how you say it.

We're looking for congruence with who you are as a person, your values, and your vision for your life and business. Communicating congruently without mixed messages involves paying attention to the tone of voice and body language.

For example, if you're trying to express yourself with clarity and power and you shrug at the end, you have just sent a mixed message. The shrug communicates some unexpressed question or hesitation. Maybe it's that you don't *really* believe what you're saying, or you don't believe it's worth expressing, or you don't expect to be taken seriously.

Another example is if you allow a tone of sarcasm to creep into your conversation. Sarcasm invites both misunderstandings and a defensive reaction from your partner.

Especially for leaders, being able to communicate congruently is critical as it enhances credibility and overall effectiveness.

CHAPTER 10

Artful Advocacy: Effectively Promoting Your Interests without Imposing Them

Thus there are both shared interests and personal interests—those that serve the partnership and the organization and those that serve you. Sometimes these interests converge—what's good for you is also good for your partner and the business.

Sometimes, what's better for you isn't so good for your partner, the business, or both. And likewise, there are times when what's good for the business or your partner isn't necessarily what serves your interests and goals.

A willingness to acknowledge, claim, and express individual and shared interests is an integral part of getting on the same page and a critical aspect of those successful conversations.

Recognizing and advocating effectively for your and the business' interests requires both sensitivity and skill. You need to be able to:
- identify your interests
- see where there's common ground
- acknowledge where interests diverge
- advocate freely for your interests without shifting into a coercive stance or shutting down your partner's interest

For example, let's refer back to Joe, the younger brother in the family business. He wants a lifestyle where he's able to travel with his kids' soccer team, make enough money to send all three of his kids to a good college, and be able to retire when he's 65.

His goal is to create enough value in the business that he and his brother can sell when they reach retirement age. But, because his brother is eight years older and nothing can be discussed, the actual plan moving forward is ambiguous. He hasn't mentioned his goals and doesn't know what his brother thinks about any of this.

Contrast that scenario with Melanie and Lori, two long-time friends and business partners who regularly talk about their life goals, their intentions for the business, and their plan to double its value. Because they're on the same page, they can sell when the market is right or when a prime opportunity emerges. They even know what each of them wants to do after the sale of the business.

Artful Advocacy: What Are the Three Critical Steps?

There are three crucial aspects to being able to articulate your interests clearly. The first is to *know* them. Again, this is where an awareness of your values comes into play.

Knowing what kind of lifestyle you want, what kind of priority you put on family life, leisure activities, recreation, travel, and so on. You need to know what matters to you to articulate and express your interests to your partner.

Self-exploration and taking full responsibility for your motives and expectations are critical at this stage. Getting clear about what you want, how it serves you, whether it benefits the business or diverges from the business's or your partner's best interest are things that you can work out, but only when you acknowledge them and place them front and center on the table.

The second aspect is *being able to talk* about your interests with clarity. And again, when you're not holding back and not waiting to get triggered to express opinions, you set the stage to advocate freely for yourself and your interests without imposing them on your partner.

Partners are often afraid to talk clearly about their interests; usually, it's because they're not following the rule of zero percent responsibility for their partner. Based on a desire to be considerate and not impose their wishes, they may not speak clearly or passionately about their interests.

In contrast, partners who fail to acknowledge and remove emotional baggage of resentment, stress, or bitterness may impose their views on their partner as though their life depended on it!

The third aspect of articulating interests is to *evaluate* them. Where can you bend? And where do you need to stand firm? This harkens back to knowing what matters to you and why, as well as knowing what matters to your partner. It's also a place for flexible, out-of-the-box thinking so you can not only reframe problems but also solve them creatively.

Many partners find it challenging to find the right balance between advocating for their position fully—without diminishing their views, and not imposing their opinions on their partner. Self-awareness, curiosity, and responsibility are again vital here, but so is having trust that your partner will advocate fully for themselves, so you don't need to worry about dominating or overpowering them.

When both partners can articulate their interests and advocate for them without imposing them, you have the recipe for a successful outcome.

CHAPTER 11

Putting the Power of Written Agreements to Work for You

W hen partners are willing and able to talk about issues to the point of agreement and then can capture that agreement in writing, they're eons ahead of those who don't. For one thing, writing out your agreement builds your muscle for addressing issues to the finish line.

Writing also clarifies your thinking and articulates what you agree to. Writing is the easiest way to see if your thinking is clear, and it's the most effective way to track where you agree and where you still differ in your views.

Writing a charter or constitution provides a documented understanding that you can refer back to. Work your way into a more comprehensive agreement by jotting down and recording your successful conversations' outcomes.

Capture your points of agreement, creating momentum, and building confidence in the process. Before you know it, you'll have pages of topics you've agreed on, and you'll be devising your long-term strategy as you go.

Topics on which to provide written documentation often include:
- Individual and shared values
- Values that shape the business vision and mission
- Vision and strategy for the business
- What kind of culture you want to create and why
- Rules of engagement when conducting business
- Expectations of yourselves and each other

- How to hold team members accountable, how to provide feedback, compensation, and other rewards
- How to manage ownership and decision-making
- How often to meet and review business initiatives
- Plans/desire for growth
- Under what circumstances to include additional family members or friends in the business and the process for doing so
- Governance issues
- Contingency plans for each of the partners
- Insurance

I've worked with families in business who included basic elements of talking with respect and civility as part of their agreement. Then, when anyone in the family slipped into disrespectful language or tone of voice, others could call them back to the standard they had agreed to earlier. It sounds simple, but some of these fundamental aspects provide the building blocks for more complex problem-solving.

Approximation toward the goal is hugely important as you get to experience a sense of progress. This is another time when an outside observer or facilitator can be beneficial as they keep the momentum going and capture the agreement's language as it's unfolding in real-time.

CHAPTER 12

Top 10 Biggest Mistakes

1. Relying on DIY and Simply Trying Harder

It's so tempting when faced with tough problems just to hunker down and work harder. It feels safer and easier than rocking the boat.

But trying harder and doing more of the same doesn't get you unstuck. There needs to be a pivot that helps you establish and maintain a better flow between you and your partner.

This pivot happens most easily with the aid of an outside perspective—other than your spouse or friend—they have their limits too!

---

2. Exhausting Yourself Trying To Change Who You Are

If you stop trusting your natural strengths and start to devalue or hold back your contributions, the business suffers. Plus, it's exhausting to continuously second guess yourself and try to 'be someone' you think would be more acceptable.

There's a constant tension involved between becoming the best leader you can be by sanding your rough edges and developing your EQ, and trying to change who you are in order to fit in or get along. The first allows you to be more fully yourself whereas the second involves diminishing your style often out of self-doubt or guilt.

Get clear about your strengths so you can let them shine, bringing your very best to the partnership and business.

3. 'Tiptoeing' in the Business More Than Ever

Ironically, partners who acknowledge that the partnership is in trouble often start tiptoeing more than ever—trying to get through each day without a major upset. They put off talking about decisions or other hot topics so as not to 'poke the bear.'

Business initiatives suffer from this. And, the tension starts rippling out to everyone in the business, making it uncomfortable for all.

More dialogue is needed, not less. It's paramount to set the stage for successful conversations so you can get off the merry-go-round and experience real resolution.

4. Hiding the Problems from Trusted Advisors

Partners often think they should know what to do when challenges in the partnership arise. There's an ingrained reluctance to be vulnerable and acknowledge problems in the leadership team.

But conflict within a partnership is a little bit like an infection in the body. It tends to fester and turn into a raging infection that threatens overall viability if it's not addressed.

As humbling or vulnerable as it might seem, it's crucial to have honest conversations with advisors sooner rather than later. They are in a much better position to help you address the issues or to help you find specialized support.

---

5. Failing to Bring in Specialized Help to Reframe Problems and Facilitate Successful Outcomes

Attorneys, accounts, financial advisors, or consultants who work with family businesses are often savvy around interpersonal dynamics. And these advisors already know the business and enjoy a considerable measure of trust.

But the advantages of these advisors can also be the limitation. Their long-standing advisor status means they're also embedded in the process. It may be hard for them to provide an unbiased and genuinely outside perspective that's specifically tailored to facilitate conversations and resolve differences.

Do yourself the favor of getting the most expert help available as quickly as possible to give yourself and your partnership the best chance of success and minimize your stress and worry along the way.

6. Not Realizing Your Great Potential to Effect Change

When you don't see your contribution to the problem, you miss seeing your huge opportunity to create solutions. In contrast, when you own the internal conflicts and recognize that at least one of the battles is *within you*, you have enormous power to influence and create change.

7. Getting Caught in the Blame Game

You might find yourself playing the blame game even without meaning to. Particularly with siblings and parents, past events can linger, creating both bitterness and resentment.

Bitterness is like a wound with a scab over it, but with all the infection still inside (it's like a scab of anger over a bunch of hurts). If you don't have a way of excising the wounds and letting them heal, you're likely to stay stuck in past resentments, allowing them to be fueled by the events of today. This is bad for partnerships and bad for business.

The only way through that is to get clear on what was the past, what's happening now, and how to deal with it effectively. Hit the easy button and get some help with this.

---

8. Giving Up: Withdrawing or 'Going It Alone'

Giving up happens along a continuum. You might think to yourself: *"we can't seem to agree on anything, so there's nothing I can do—I can't move forward in any direction."* This paralysis deprives your partner and the business of your necessary talent and effort.

The opposite thinking goes like this: *"we can't seem to agree on anything, so I'm just going to move forward and do what I think is right."* 'Going it alone' means there's no unified strategy for the team to pursue.

Monitoring your level of resignation is essential, so it doesn't get out of hand and further divide the partnership and stall the business. Setting the stage for successful conversations is critical.

9. Not Taking Time to Master New Patterns So They Become Second Nature

Essential skills needed for a successful partnership don't develop overnight. Remembering to use The Threshold Technique, to implement the five C's for successful conversations, and to tend your underlying belief system is a process.

When these skills are mastered, they genuinely do become second nature. But until then, tenaciousness is key. It's essential to practice and keep these skills top of mind by giving attention to personal and interpersonal development every week. It's rewarding!

10. Failing to Calculate the Cost of Not Being on the Same Page

When a frog is in water that's gradually heated to boiling, a certain tolerance develops. In partnerships, it's easy to lose sight of the tremendous cost of not being on the same page and not look downstream to see the effects on the employees and take into account the cumulative impact.

So maybe you're experiencing higher levels of stress, health challenges, less quality sleep, more strained relationships, but perhaps you've grown accustomed to it and have failed to calculate the impact.

Getting clear about what this is costing you and the business in terms of decreased engagement, motivation, ability to execute strategy, ability to be nimble and act on opportunities, to deliver the highest quality service, etc., is a huge spur toward taking smart and immediate action.

Long-Term Profitability with Same Page Leadership

Breathe Easy and Enjoy Stress-Free Conversations

When you and your partner are on the same page, you can breathe! You no longer carry around the weight and tension of a strained partnership. You don't have to dread making decisions because you know you can talk about things and work them out without unproductive heated debates or days of silence.

When you have honest conversations with your partner and truly get on the same page, you'll not only survive in your partnership; you'll thrive!

Transform Your Partnership from Brittle to Resilient

Resilience is the ability to bounce back. It implies strength and stretchiness—a certain amount of give.

Contrast that with the tense experience of walking on eggshells.

When you and your partner can resolve significant issues between you, articulate interests clearly and without fear, and know you have each other's back, you can tackle the challenges of running a business with the confidence of having a resilient partnership.

Go with the Current, Not Against It

When your roles and responsibilities are sorted according to your natural strengths, you can enjoy working in your zone of genius, knowing your partner is doing the same. It can feel as effortless as paddling downstream.

Additionally, it promotes a culture where everyone in the organization can use their natural talents and do work that energizes rather than depletes them.

Enjoy Freedom to Be in Your Own Lane

Another advantage of having trust restored and roles and responsibilities well-defined is that each of you can enjoy the autonomy of working in your own lane. You can combine the results of your efforts, rather than getting caught in redundancy that's born in mistrust.

Enact the Vision of Your Business with Confidence

When the challenges inherent in any business partnership no longer derail you, you can devote your time, talent, and energies to bring your business vision into full reality.

You now can do this without friction and with a great deal of confidence because you and your partner have taken the time to get on the same page and resolve potentially destructive differences.

Take a minute to congratulate yourselves and appreciate how you've been truly audacious, gracious, and tenacious in the pursuit of your goals.

Chart Your Course to Serve Your Vision— Two Viable Scenarios

Imagine for a moment scenario number one. You're showing up as the leader you want to be, knowing you're doing what you need to do to enact the vision you and your partner share. Imagine feeling good at the end of the day, going home to your family, or meeting up with friends and *actually* being there— not preoccupied with the stuff that used to eat away at you.

Imagine yourself carrying out your business role with confidence and self-respect and having the ripple effects of this flow through the entire business. You are living the life you designed and are tending your partnership and the business, functioning on the same page and enjoying the flow of your profitable business.

Now imagine for a moment scenario number two. Suppose that you decide with clarity and freedom that this business no longer meets your goals and vision for your life, and you find a way to exit or bring closure to the company. Imagine that you find a way to do this that honors the dreams and vision you had at the start—no small task but so very worth it.

You take the lessons you learned and the resilience you built and bring that into your next exciting endeavor!

Contrast that with feeling desperate to find a way out of the business, taking a loss, or leaving on bad terms, all because you couldn't see the path of how to work things out. The stakes are high. Play your hand well. Use this (or someone else's) roadmap and gift yourself any assistance you need or desire.

Create Ease in Your Business and Partnership

If you're reading this book, you know there are issues to solve and that the time is now. Business is challenging enough without having partner conflicts undermining your efforts and diminishing your vision (not to mention affecting your health and sleep!)

The number one regret I hear from business owners on the other side of a conflict is that they didn't get help for the partnership and/or didn't get it early enough. Once they saw how much better things could be with some outside counsel, they wondered why they waited so long.

Don't spend another day mired in the status quo, hoping it will get better yet deep down knowing it won't. Your life can be so much easier than what it is now.

NEXT STEPS

I hope this book has sparked new hope and has given you a roadmap for the journey ahead. Whenever you're ready, here are three ways we can help:

1. Subscribe to the Audacious Leaders Podcast. https://nancyjonker.com/podcast

2. Get your *Leadership Effectiveness Scorecard* and discover hidden areas of potential to catapult your leadership to the next level. https://QuizLeaders.com

3. Have you ever felt like you're rowing the boat forward, while your partners are rowing in the opposite direction...with bigger oars? Not only are you not getting anywhere, you might be going backward. Eventually, the boat will sink.

    If that's you, our Audacious Leaders M.O. Program is specifically designed for you. We help partners who are stuck to finally start communicating, get rowing in the same direction, grow the business, and find peace, ease, and happiness in the partnership again.

    If you're ready to fix your partnership, email me right now at nancy@drjonker.com and put "Audacious Leaders" in the subject line. I'll get you all the details without delay.

ABOUT THE AUTHOR

Since 1989, Nancy Jonker, PhD has used her training in clinical psychology to serve individuals, partners, and families helping them have successful conversations so they can get on the same page and create a clear path forward.

Nancy is the author of the best selling book *Get Your Power On*, is host of the Audacious Leaders Podcast, and is the creator of Audacious Leaders M.O. Program, a method to help leaders use their natural talents, hone their communication skills, and catapult their results to create the life and business they enjoy.